U.S.A. TRAVEL GUIDES

MAINE

BY ANN HEINRICHS • ILLUSTRATED BY MATT KANIA

The Child's World

childsworld.com

Published by The Child's World®
1980 Lookout Drive • Mankato, MN 56003-1705
800-599-READ • www.childsworld.com

Photo Credits

Photographs ©: Kristy Viera/Shutterstock Images, cover,
1; Kristi Rugg/National Park Service, 7; Christopher
Badzioch/iStockphoto, 8; Meagan Racey/U.S. Fish
and Wildlife Service, 11; Andre Jenny Stock Connection
Worldwide/Newscom, 12, 35; Felix Lipov/Shutterstock
Images, 15; Pat Wellenbac/Maine Maritime Museum/
AP Images, 16; Petty Officer 2nd Class Rob Simpson/
U.S. Coast Guard, 19; iStockphoto, 20, 27; Carol M.
Highsmith/Carol M. Highsmith Archive/Library of
Congress, 23, 32; Jeff Greenberg 6 of 6/Alamy, 24;
Thos. Moser, 28; National Park Service, 31; Shutterstock
Images, 37 (top), 37 (bottom)

ISBN 9781503819597
LCCN 2016961137

Printing

Printed in the United States of America
PA02334

Ann Heinrichs is the author of more than 100 books for children and young adults. She has also enjoyed successful careers as a children's book editor and an advertising copywriter. Ann grew up in Fort Smith, Arkansas, and lives in Chicago, Illinois.

About the Author
Ann Heinrichs

Matt Kania loves maps and, as a kid, dreamed of making them. In school he studied geography and cartography, and today he makes maps for a living. Matt's favorite thing about drawing maps is learning about the places they represent. Many of the maps he has created can be found in books, magazines, videos, Web sites, and public places.

About the
Map Illustrator
Matt Kania

*On the cover: The Portland Head Light is
on the shore of Fort Williams Park.*

OUR MAINE TRIP

MAINE

What will you do in Maine today? Meet sea captains and woodworkers? Tie sailors' knots and eat lobsters? Watch people turn wood into paper? Climb a lighthouse? Or sneak up on moose in the woods?

Why pick and choose? Let's do it all! Just follow the dotted line. Or skip around. Either way, you're in for a great trip. Just remember—having fun is the Maine thing! Now, buckle up and hang on tight. We're on our way!

WELCOME TO
MAINE

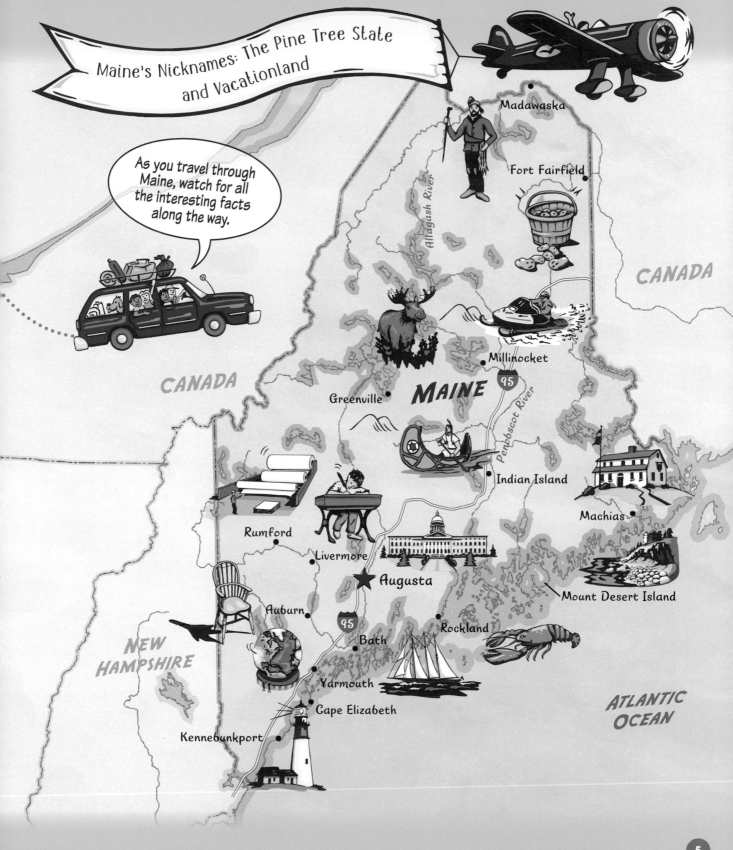

Lowest Temperature: Big Black River January 16, 2009 -50°F (-46°C)

Highest Temperature: North Bridgton July 10, 1911 105°F (41°C)

HIGHEST AND LOWEST POINTS
HIGHEST: Mount Katahdin at 5,267 feet (1,606 m)
LOWEST: Sea level along the Atlantic Ocean

Are we in Acadia National Park? Then let's go see Thunder Hole! It's a rocky place where water crashes in. It's so loud, it sounds like thunder!

West Quoddy Head is the country's easternmost point. Stand there at sunrise. You'll be the first person in the country to see the sun come up!

Two of Maine's major rivers are the Penobscot and Kennebec rivers. Both flow south into the Atlantic Ocean.

ACADIA NATIONAL PARK

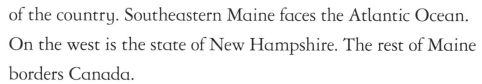

Acadia National Park is rough and wild. Just stand on its rocky cliffs. Look out, and there's the sea. Water comes crashing in with a great roar!

Most of this park is on Mount Desert Island. That's one of many islands off the coast. Maine is on the northeastern tip of the country. Southeastern Maine faces the Atlantic Ocean. On the west is the state of New Hampshire. The rest of Maine borders Canada.

Much of Maine's coast is rocky. But there are sandy beaches, too. Little fishing villages lie along the shore. Away from the coast, the land rises higher. Mountains cover much of northwestern Maine.

Catch beautiful glimpses of Maine's coast at Acadia National Park.

MOOSE MAINEA IN GREENVILLE

Explore the Moosehead Trails. Canoe on Moose River. Run in the Moose Mainea 5K. You're celebrating Moose Mainea in Greenville!

Moose Mainea honors a beloved Maine animal—the moose! Thousands of big moose live in Maine. Deer, bears, and bobcats live there, too. So do foxes, rabbits, and squirrels.

All these animals have good places to hide. They make their homes in the deep forests. They're lucky to live in Maine. Why? Because forests cover most of the state!

The coastal waters are full of sea life. Lobsters and clams are some common shellfish. Maine's fish include Atlantic herring, salmon, cod, and flounder.

You might even see a moose when you stop by Greenville's Moose Mainea!

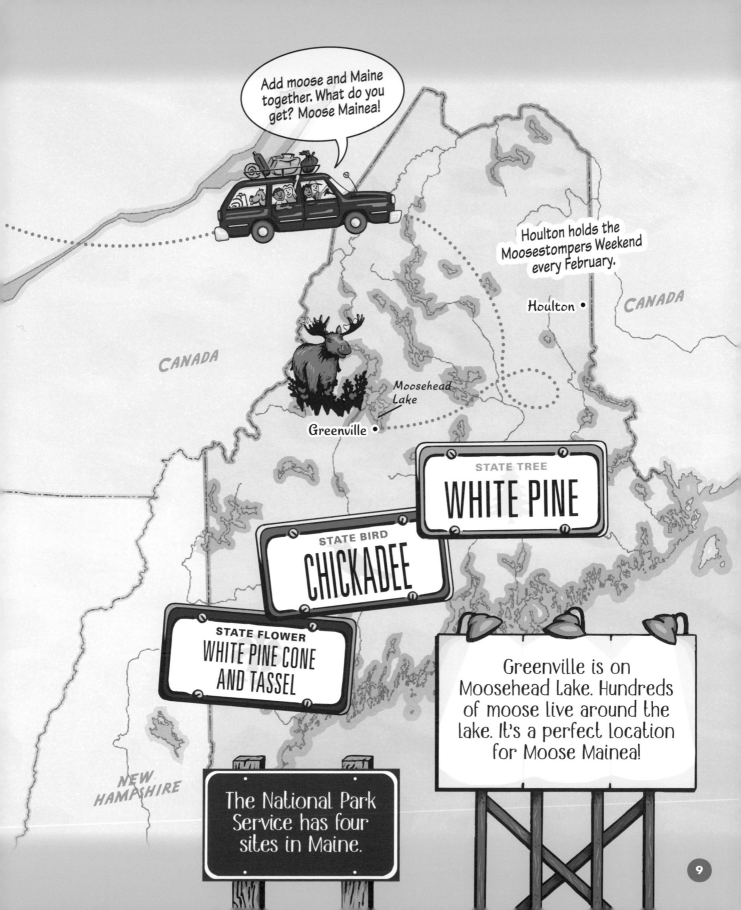

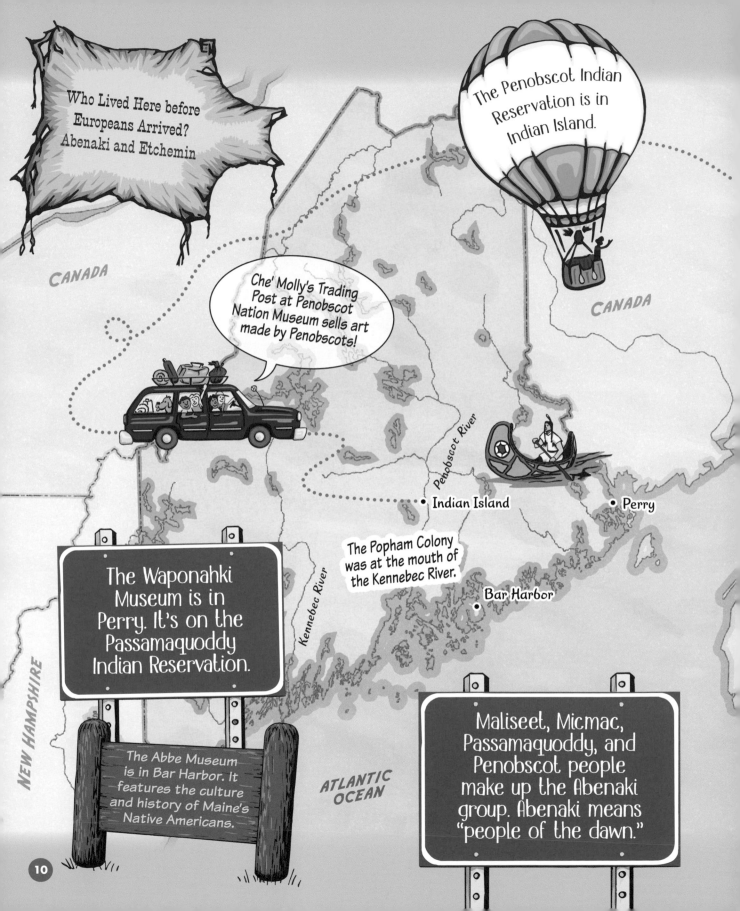

INDIAN ISLAND'S PENOBSCOT NATION MUSEUM

The Penobscots live in eastern Maine. The Penobscot Nation Museum shares their history.

Historically, Penobscots made canoes with birch tree bark. They also made decorated clothes and headdresses for ceremonies. You'll see all these things at the museum. You'll also see contemporary art.

English settlers sailed to Maine in 1607. They set up the Popham **Colony**. But they left the next year. More **colonists** came in the 1620s and stayed. Maine became part of the Massachusetts Bay Colony.

Colonists and Native Americans fought many battles. Both sides wanted the land as their own. In the end, the United States drove Native Americans off their land. Some Native Americans were sent to **reservations**.

The Penobscot Nation has joined the Penobscot River Restoration Trust to restore the population of 11 native species of fish in the Penobscot River. Two dams were torn down to help the fish thrive.

BURNHAM TAVERN AND THE REVOLUTIONARY WAR

Thirteen British colonies grew up along North America's Atlantic coast. The colonists came to hate British taxes. They decided to fight for freedom from British rule. This fight is called the Revolutionary War (1775–1783).

One night, colonists met in Machias's Burnham Tavern. They planned to capture the British ship *Margaretta*. And they did! In the end, the colonies won the war. They became the United States of America.

You can visit Burnham Tavern today. You'll see old iron pots by the fireplace. That's where dinners were cooked!

Burnham Tavern was one of the most important homes of the American Revolution.

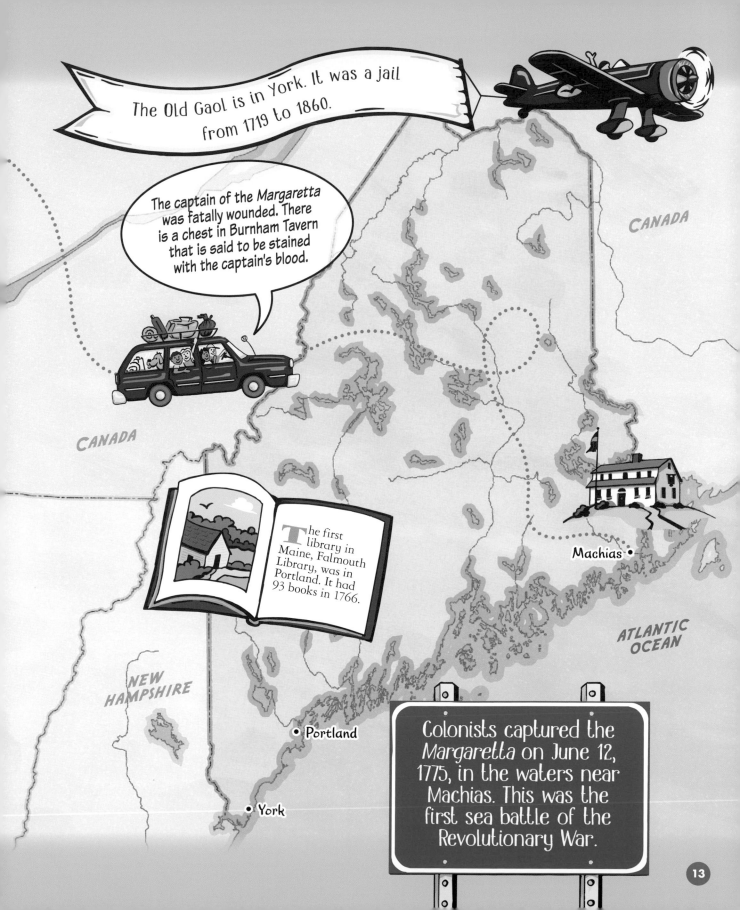

The Old Gaol is in York. It was a jail from 1719 to 1860.

The captain of the *Margaretta* was fatally wounded. There is a chest in Burnham Tavern that is said to be stained with the captain's blood.

CANADA

CANADA

The first library in Maine, Falmouth Library, was in Portland. It had 93 books in 1766.

Machias

ATLANTIC OCEAN

NEW HAMPSHIRE

• Portland

• York

Colonists captured the *Margaretta* on June 12, 1775, in the waters near Machias. This was the first sea battle of the Revolutionary War.

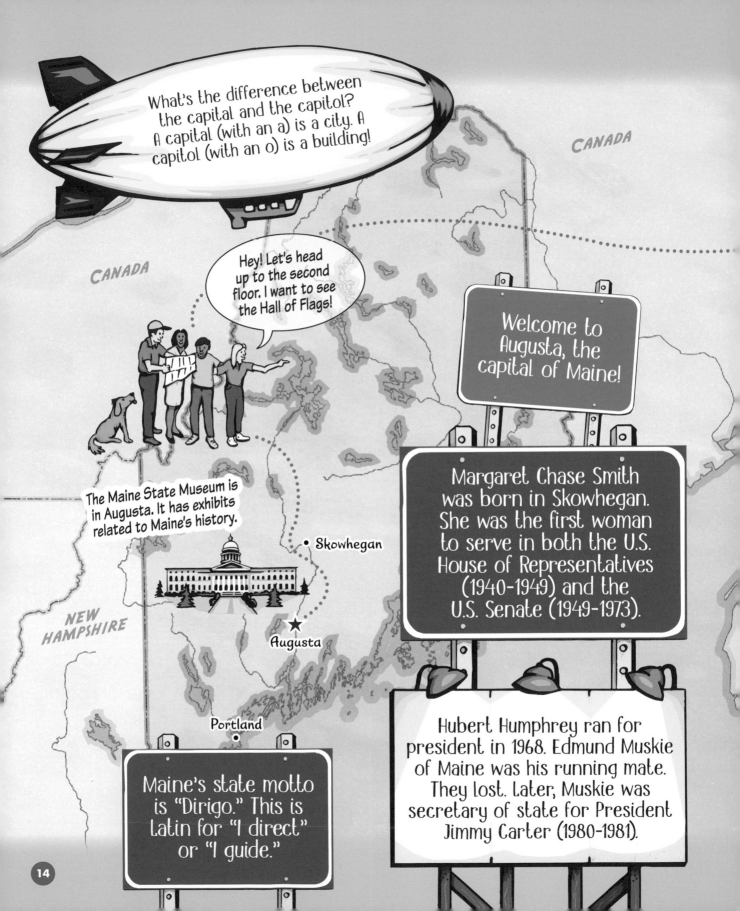

What's the difference between the capital and the capitol? A capital (with an a) is a city. A capitol (with an o) is a building!

Hey! Let's head up to the second floor. I want to see the Hall of Flags!

CANADA

CANADA

The Maine State Museum is in Augusta. It has exhibits related to Maine's history.

NEW HAMPSHIRE

Skowhegan

Augusta

Portland

Welcome to Augusta, the capital of Maine!

Margaret Chase Smith was born in Skowhegan. She was the first woman to serve in both the U.S. House of Representatives (1940-1949) and the U.S. Senate (1949-1973).

Hubert Humphrey ran for president in 1968. Edmund Muskie of Maine was his running mate. They lost. Later, Muskie was secretary of state for President Jimmy Carter (1980-1981).

Maine's state motto is "Dirigo." This is Latin for "I direct" or "I guide."

THE STATE CAPITOL IN AUGUSTA

Maine used to be part of Massachusetts. But Maine broke away in 1820. It became a state of its own. Portland was the first state capital. But Portland was on the coast. **Politicians** wanted a capital closer to the state's center. They chose Augusta in 1827. There they built the state government building—the capitol.

Inside the capitol are important government offices. Maine's government has three branches. One branch makes state laws. Another branch carries out the laws. It's headed by the governor. The third branch is made up of judges. They decide whether laws have been broken.

The first American-born architect, Charles Bulfinch, designed Maine's capitol building.

THE MAINE MARITIME MUSEUM IN BATH

Do you love ships and the sea? Then you'll love the Maine **Maritime** Museum in Bath. You'll learn how Mainers built and sailed ships. You'll try your hand at tying sailors' knots. Go explore the shipyard. Then hop aboard a boat. You'll coast down the Kennebec River.

Fishing and sailing are old **traditions** in Maine. Many Mainers sailed out to sea in big ships. Others sailed smaller boats close to shore. The sailors caught lobsters, fish, and even whales.

Shipbuilding became an important **industry**. The thick pine forests provided wood for the ships. Maine's shipbuilders made sturdy ships for fishing. They also built warships for the U.S. Navy.

The Maine Maritime Museum has all sorts of ship-related artifacts, including historic ship artwork.

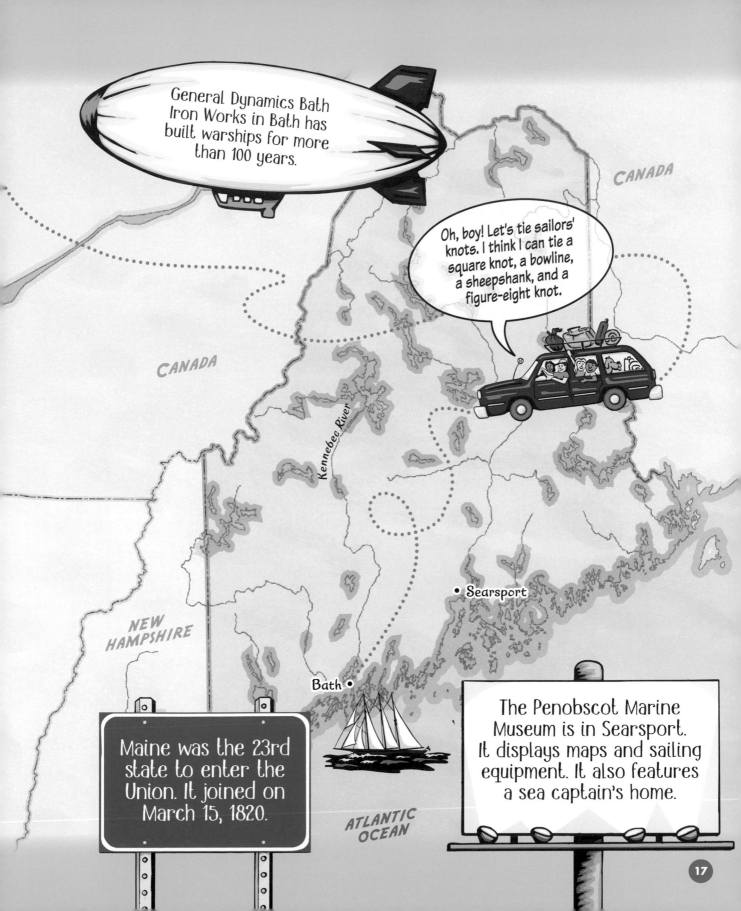

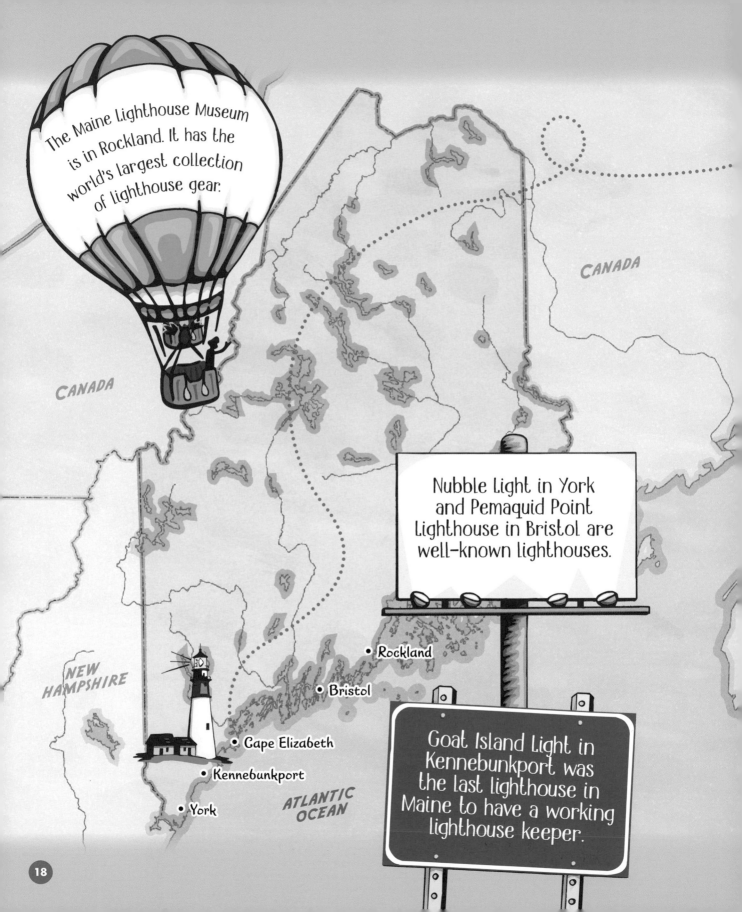

The Maine Lighthouse Museum is in Rockland. It has the world's largest collection of lighthouse gear.

CANADA

CANADA

Nubble Light in York and Pemaquid Point Lighthouse in Bristol are well-known lighthouses.

NEW HAMPSHIRE

• Rockland

• Bristol

• Cape Elizabeth

• Kennebunkport

ATLANTIC OCEAN

• York

Goat Island Light in Kennebunkport was the last lighthouse in Maine to have a working lighthouse keeper.

Nubble Light got its name because it stands on a small lump, or nubble, of land!

More than 60 lighthouses rise along Maine's coast. Their lights guide ships safely back to shore. Lighthouse keepers used to tend the lighthouses. They kept lanterns burning in the tower.

Most of Maine's lighthouses still work today. You can climb some of them. Their lights are electric now. Most also have foghorns. The horns blast loudly when it's foggy. Boats can follow the sound back to shore.

Ask Mainers which lighthouse is the most famous. Many will say it's Portland Head Light. It looks out from Cape Elizabeth. Built in 1791, it's Maine's oldest lighthouse.

The Portland Head Light was first lit in 1791. Today, the Keeper's Quarters are a museum.

ROCKLAND'S MAINE LOBSTER FESTIVAL

Are you good at keeping your balance? Then check out the Maine Lobster Festival in Rockland. You could win the lobster crate race! Lobster crates are boxes for holding lobsters.

How does the race work? Lobster crates are tied together in the water. The crates make a kind of race track. Racers run across the crates. Who's the winner? Whoever covers the most crates before falling in!

People eat lots of lobster at this festival. Many other coastal towns have lobster festivals, too. It's no wonder. Maine catches more lobsters than any other state!

You'll see lobsters everywhere at the Maine Lobster Festival!

THE LIVING HISTORY CENTER IN LIVERMORE

Many Mainers in the 1800s were farmers. They plowed their fields with ox-drawn plows. They grew crops and raised cows for milk. They gathered maple **sap** and made sugar.

Would you like to see these farm activities? Stop by the Washburn-Norlands Living History Center in Livermore. You can spend a weekend there. You'll help out with farm chores. You'll even attend classes in the old schoolhouse.

Maine also developed many industries. Mills, or water-powered factories, were built beside rivers. The mills made cotton and wool cloth. Maine was also known for its leather goods.

Israel and Martha Washburn raised ten children on the Norlands farm in the 1800s.

Do you like potatoes? Then check out the Maine Potato Blossom Festival in Fort Fairfield. You can enter the potato-picking contest. Then wrestle a friend in a pool of mashed potatoes!

Potatoes are the state's top crop. Maine's potato farmers grow millions of bushels a year!

Apples are Maine's leading fruit. Wild blueberries are important, too. Maine grows more of them than any other state.

What about chickens and cows? Plenty of them live on Maine's farms. Eggs and milk are valuable farm products.

Hurry up! Pick the potatoes as fast as you can, or you might lose the potato-picking contest!

Machias holds a blueberry festival every August.

CANADA

What a potato festival! It's got a rubber duck race and a pet show!

Aroostook County

• Fort Fairfield

Houlton •

CANADA

Most of Maine's potatoes are grown in Aroostook County. That's where Maine's potato festivals are held.

Many state **agricultural** fairs are held throughout Maine each fall.

Machias •

ATLANTIC OCEAN

What Does Maine Raise?
Potatoes, eggs, and milk

Houlton celebrates Potato Feast Days in August.

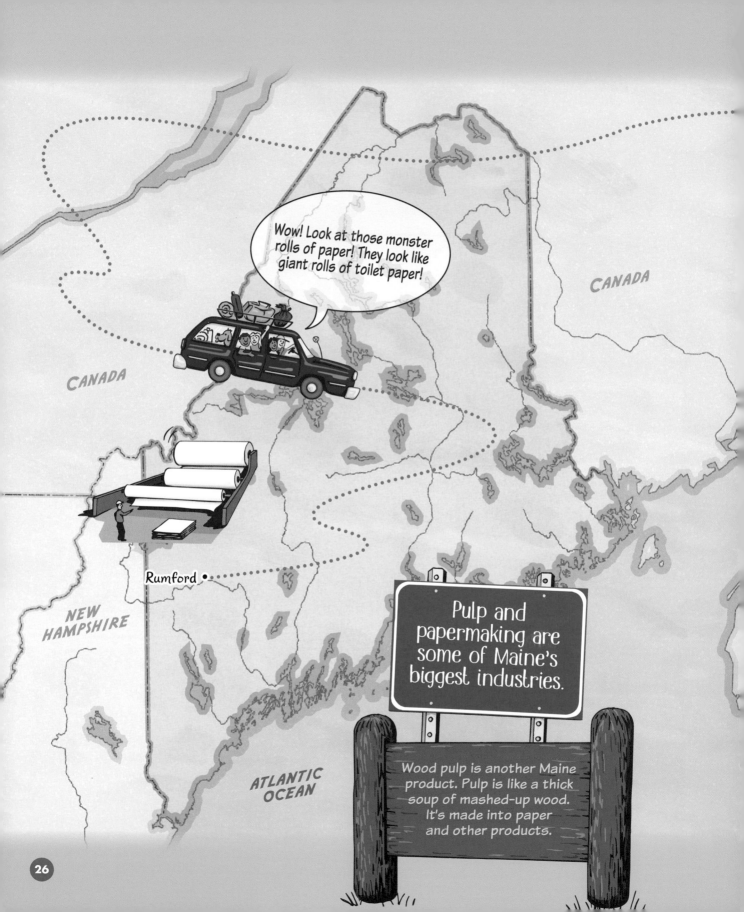

Many paper mills are at work in Maine. Just stop by Catalyst Paper's Rumford Mill in Rumford. Machines buzz away. They cut and grind wood. Then they turn wood chips into paper!

Papermaking became a big industry in Maine. Thousands of forest trees now go to paper mills. The mills turn out many products. Can you guess what some of them are?

Paper mills make cardboard boxes and paper sacks. Then there's the paper you write on. And don't forget books and newspapers. They all began as trees!

The Rumford Mill employs hundreds of people.

AUBURN'S WOOD WORKSHOP

Look at your chair or desk. Were they made by machines? Probably. But visit the Thomas Moser workshop in Auburn. You'll watch people making wood furniture by hand. You'll see them cut, glue, and sand the wood. They end up with beautiful chairs and other furniture.

Maine's wood industry has always been important. Mills throughout the state saw logs into boards. Those boards might become houses or furniture.

Maine makes all kinds of things with wood. Companies in Maine use wood to make toys, tools, and instruments!

A craftsman works at the Thomas Moser workshop.

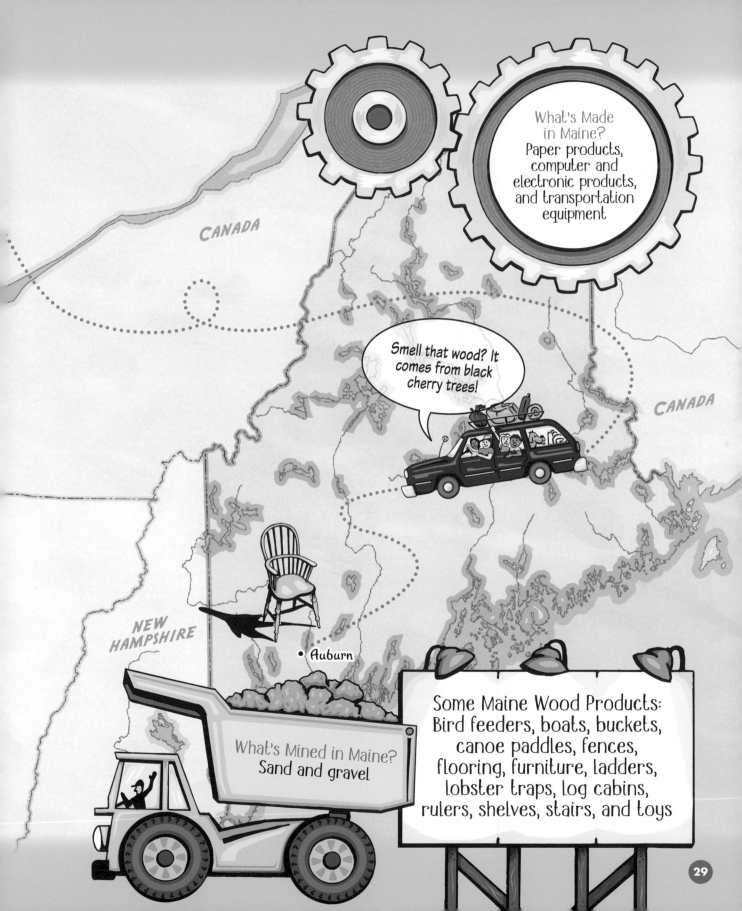

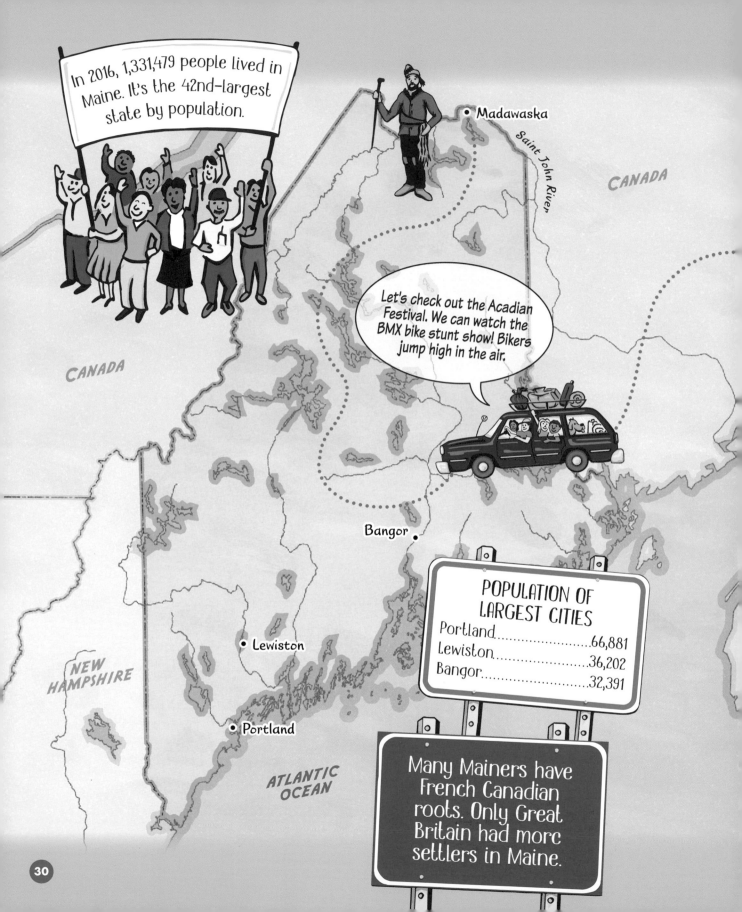

In 2016, 1,331,479 people lived in Maine. It's the 42nd-largest state by population.

Madawaska

Saint John River

CANADA

CANADA

Let's check out the Acadian Festival. We can watch the BMX bike stunt show! Bikers jump high in the air.

Bangor

POPULATION OF LARGEST CITIES
Portland................................66,881
Lewiston..............................36,202
Bangor.................................32,391

Lewiston

NEW HAMPSHIRE

Portland

ATLANTIC OCEAN

Many Mainers have French Canadian roots. Only Great Britain had more settlers in Maine.

THE ACADIAN FESTIVAL IN MADAWASKA

Madawaska is the northernmost town in Maine. Just across the Saint John River is Canada! Most people in Madawaska are Acadian. Acadia was a French colony in Canada. The British drove the Acadians out in 1755. Many Acadians went to live in Louisiana. But some settled in Maine.

Now Madawaska holds the Acadian Festival every year. People act out the Acadians' arrival in Maine. Then comes supper with beans and ham, music, and games. People wear Acadian costumes, and many speak French. Acadians are just one of Maine's ethnic groups. Some Mainers have roots in England or Ireland. Settlers came from Germany, Sweden, and many other countries.

Stop by the Acadian Landing Site while you're at the Acadian Festival. It's marked by a big marble cross.

THE KATAHDIN WINTERFEST

Grab your sled for the kids' sled race. Go ice fishing with your whole family. Watch hundreds of snowmobiles in races and parades. Are you hungry? Try the traditional Maine baked-bean supper. It's the Katahdin Area Winterfest in Millinocket!

This is one of Maine's fun winter festivals. Many other events celebrate fishing, boating, or food.

Mainers enjoy the outdoors. They go skiing or snowmobiling in the winter. In warmer weather, they enjoy swimming and sailing. Some people like climbing. They might climb mountains or rocky sea cliffs. It's great to look out from the top!

The Katahdin Area is near Mount Katahdin, the northernmost part of the Appalachian Trail.

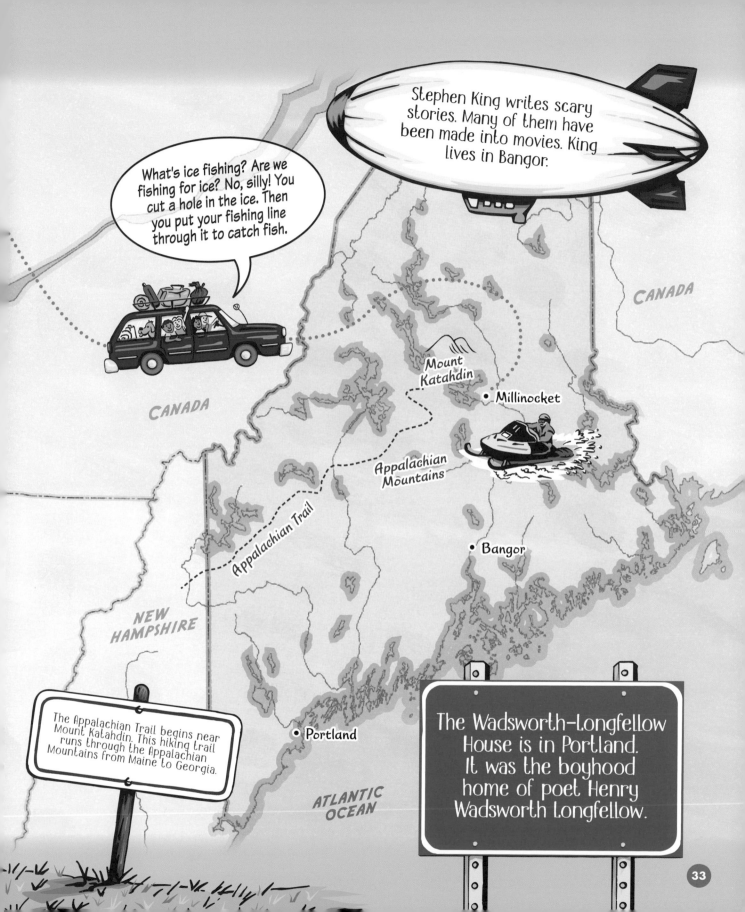

Eartha is as tall as a four-story building.

The Earth takes 24 hours to rotate, or turn around. Each full turn creates a day. Eartha rotates in 18 minutes!

CANADA

CANADA

NEW HAMPSHIRE

One inch (2.5 cm) on Eartha is equal to 1 million inches (2,540,000 cm) on Earth!

• Yarmouth

Eartha weighs more than 5,600 pounds (2,540 kg).

MEET EARTHA, THE GIANT GLOBE

Have you seen a globe of the Earth? Well, you've never seen one like Eartha. It's the world's largest **rotating** globe. It turns around just like our planet does.

You can see Eartha at Yarmouth's DeLorme Company. This mapmaking company built the globe. The idea was to fill people with wonder. They'd see how everyone on Earth is connected.

Suppose you wanted to hug Eartha. You'd need lots of other kids to help you. You'd all join hands around the globe. How many kids would it take? More than 30! What a hug!

It took over a year to collect the mapping data needed to make Eartha!

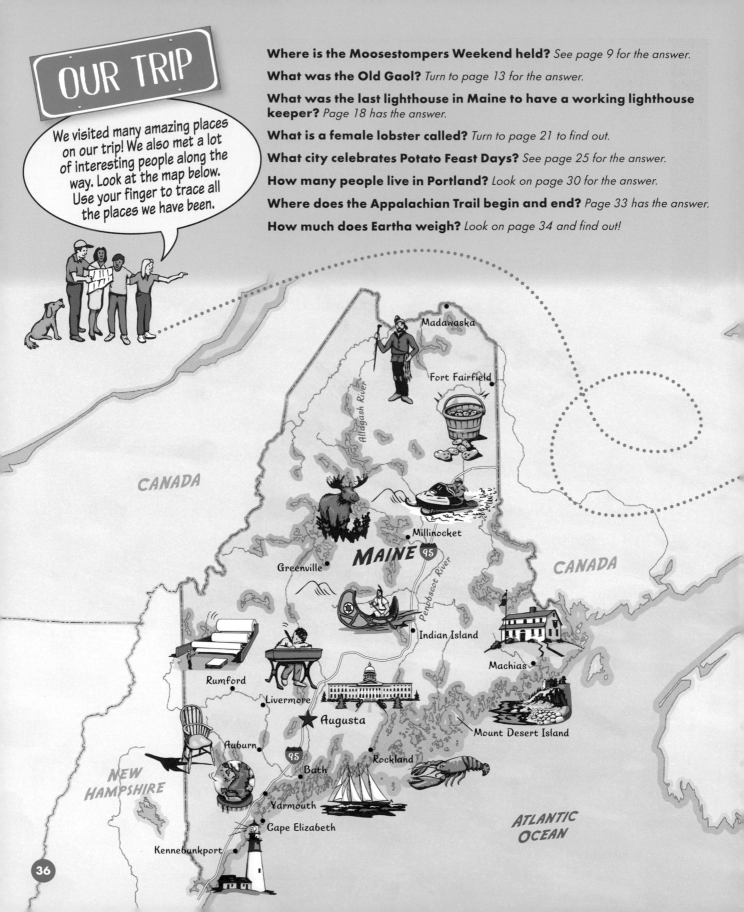

OUR TRIP

We visited many amazing places on our trip! We also met a lot of interesting people along the way. Look at the map below. Use your finger to trace all the places we have been.

Where is the Moosestompers Weekend held? *See page 9 for the answer.*

What was the Old Gaol? *Turn to page 13 for the answer.*

What was the last lighthouse in Maine to have a working lighthouse keeper? *Page 18 has the answer.*

What is a female lobster called? *Turn to page 21 to find out.*

What city celebrates Potato Feast Days? *See page 25 for the answer.*

How many people live in Portland? *Look on page 30 for the answer.*

Where does the Appalachian Trail begin and end? *Page 33 has the answer.*

How much does Eartha weigh? *Look on page 34 and find out!*

Madawaska

Fort Fairfield

Allagash River

CANADA

MAINE 95

Millinocket

Greenville

Penobscot River

CANADA

Indian Island

Machias

Rumford

Livermore

Augusta

Mount Desert Island

Auburn

95

Rockland

Bath

NEW HAMPSHIRE

Yarmouth

Cape Elizabeth

ATLANTIC OCEAN

Kennebunkport

State flag

State seal

STATE SYMBOLS

State animal: Moose

State berry: Wild blueberry

State bird: Black-capped chickadee

State cat: Maine coon cat

State fish: Landlocked salmon

State flower: White pine cone and tassel

State fossil: *Pertica quadrifaria,* a primitive plant

State gemstone: Tourmaline

State herb: Wintergreen

State insect: Honeybee

State soil: Chesuncook soil series

State tree: White pine

State vessel: The arctic exploration schooner *Bowdoin*

STATE SONG

"STATE OF MAINE SONG"

Words and music by Roger Vinton Snow

Grand State of Maine, proudly we sing
To tell your glories to the land,
To shout your praises till the echoes ring.
Should fate unkind send us to roam,
The scent of the fragrant pines,
The tang of the salty sea will call us
    home.

Chorus:
Oh, Pine Tree State,
Your woods, fields and hills,
Your lakes, streams and rockbound coast
Will ever fill our hearts with thrills,
And tho' we seek far and wide
Our search will be in vain,
To find a fairer spot on earth
Than Maine! Maine! Maine!

That was a great trip! We have traveled all over Maine! There are a few places that we didn't have time for, though. Next time, we plan to visit the Seaside Trolley Museum in Kennebunkport. Visitors can view the National Collection of Streetcars. Trolley tours of the area are available, too.

FAMOUS PEOPLE

Bean, L. L. (1872–1967), apparel company founder

Bradley, Milton (1836–1911), early childhood educator

Craven, Ricky (1966–), NASCAR racer

Dix, Dorothea (1802–1887), social reformer

Ford, John (1894–1973), film director

Hussey, Curtis (1981–), wrestler known as Fandango

Kendrick, Anna (1985–), actress

King, Stephen (1947–), author

Longfellow, Henry Wadsworth (1807–1882), poet

McCloskey, Robert (1914–2003), children's author and illustrator

Millay, Edna St. Vincent (1892–1950), poet

Morse, Marston (1892–1977), mathematician

Piston, Walter (1894–1976), composer

Samuelson, Joan Benoit (1957–), Olympic distance runner

Smith, Margaret Chase (1897–1995), politician

Stowe, Harriet Beecher (1811–1896) author

Tyler, Liv (1977–), actor

White, E. B. (1899–1985), children's author

WORDS TO KNOW

agricultural (ag-rih-KUL-chur-uhl) having to do with farming

colonists (KOL-uh-nists) people who settle a new land for their home country

colony (KOL-uh-nee) a land with ties to a mother country

industry (IN-duh-stree) a type of business

maritime (MA-ruh-time) having to do with travel and work at sea

politicians (pol-uh-TISH-uhnz) leaders involved in government

reservations (rez-ur-VAY-shuhnz) places set aside for a special use, such as a home for Native Americans

rotating (ROH-tate-ing) turning around on a center point

sap (SAP) a sticky juice that oozes from some kinds of trees

traditions (truh-DISH-uhnz) customs followed for many years

TO LEARN MORE

IN THE LIBRARY

Connors, Kathleen. *Acadia National Park*. New York, NY: Gareth Stevens Publishing, 2016.

Koontz, Robin. *Maine: The Pine Tree State*. New York, NY: PowerKids Press, 2011.

ON THE WEB

Visit our Web site for links about Maine:

childsworld.com/links

Note to Parents, Teachers, and Librarians: We routinely verify our Web links to make sure they are safe and active sites. So encourage your readers to check them out!

PLACES TO VISIT OR CONTACT

Maine Historical Society

mainehistory.org
489 Congress Street
Portland, ME 04101
207/774-1822
For more information about the history of Maine

Maine Office of Tourism

visitmaine.com
59 State House Station
Augusta, ME 04333
888/624-6345
For more information about traveling in Maine

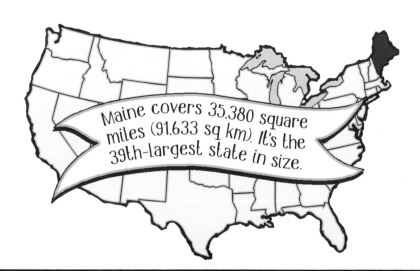

Maine covers 35,380 square miles (91,633 sq km). It's the 39th-largest state in size.

INDEX

Bye, Pine Tree State.
We had a great time.
We'll come back soon!